The Peach Thief

By Maggie Vaughn

Ashley and Grandad Keith got set up for film night.

"We can eat a sweet treat while the film is on," said Ashley.

Ashley reached for the dish of peaches.

But it was empty. No peaches!

We need to track down the peach thief!

Ashley ran to her puppy, Chief.

"Have you seen the peaches, Chief?" she said.

But Chief was sleeping and dreaming of beef.

Grandad Keith peeked up the chimney.

“It is squeaky clean. No peaches!” he called.

"Where are they?" said Ashley.

"Beats me!" said Grandad Keith.

Mum sat in the study
with a cup of tea
and an empty dish!

Mum, I see peach
on your cheek!
You are the peach thief!

Mum put her hand on her cheek.

"No, but we have heaps
of peach chunks
in the deep freeze!" said Mum.

Ashley gave Mum a big smile.

Grandad Keith made drinks
with peach chunks and cream.

Ashley was so happy
with the film feast!

CHECKING FOR MEANING

1. What are two places where Grandad Keith and Ashley looked for the missing peaches? *(Literal)*
2. Was Chief awake when Ashley asked him about the peaches? *(Literal)*
3. How did Ashley know Mum was the peach thief? *(Inferential)*

EXTENDING VOCABULARY

treat	Read the word *treat*. How are treats different from other foods? How often should you eat a treat?
track down	What did Ashley and Grandad Keith do when they tracked down the peach thief? What is another way to say *track down*?
squeaky clean	What does it mean if something is *squeaky clean*? Is it kind of clean or very clean?

MOVING BEYOND THE TEXT

1. Mum probably should have shared the peaches with Ashley and Grandad Keith. Tell me about a time you shared with someone.
2. What is your favourite treat to eat?
3. What other foods might people eat when they watch a movie?
4. What are some other activities Ashley and Grandad Keith might do together?

TIME TO WRITE

Write about a time you found something you had lost in an unexpected place.

PRACTICE WORDS